The Paper Trail: Useful Charts to Organize Your Writing

The Writer's Toolbox Series

by Lee E. Cart

For all my writer friends, old and new

Also by Lee E. Cart

The Cracker Book: Artisanal Crackers for Every Occasion

The Paper Trail: Useful Charts to Organize Your Writing

The Writer's Toolbox Series

Introduction

Many of you may be wondering why you need a set of charts to keep your writing organized. After all, you have your computer with all its various files. Or you use some app online that keeps everything tidy, so what's the point of having paper copies? Having paper copies just adds more clutter to your desk, uses paper and ink, and duplicates what you may already have out there in the Internet.

That's what I thought until the day my computer, with all its lovely files, suddenly crashed! I have to admit, I panicked. Instantly, I had no access to anything, none of my work in progress, none of my account information, no way to access the Internet, nothing. And to make matters worse, it happened on a Saturday night, when my local computer fix-it place was closed. So, I waited impatiently and unhappily through a very long Sunday and promptly took my laptop to my local computer guy first thing Monday morning.

He had other clients ahead of me and was unable to take a look at my nonfunctioning computer until late in the afternoon, so Monday was another very long day, with no access to my stuff! I spent the afternoon researching types of computers, processors, hard drives, etc. just in case my gut feeling that I needed a new laptop was true. Tuesday morning, I called the minute the shop opened. My computer was history. I definitely needed a new one. So my husband and I jumped in the car and headed towards the nearest shops, about forty-five minutes away. After multiple stops, I finally came home with a new machine and all my old files on a portable hard drive. I spent a good part of the evening uploading the files, downloading the programs to run them, and setting up the computer to my personal preferences. And learning how to use a new operating system! Finally, on Wednesday, after a very deep breath, I was able to get back to work.

All of which got me to thinking; what if I had had at least some of my client information written down on paper? That way, I could have done some work by hand while I waited for the verdict on my old computer. And I could have reduced my stress level because I would have known that not all of my information was tied up in an electronic box that refused to do anything other than hum oddly and project a very black screen.

One thing led to another, and I started creating charts to use in my freelance business. Then I realized that if I found them useful, some of my writer friends would probably find them helpful, too. And so, *The Paper Trail* came into being.

I've included a brief explanation of how each chart is to be used and then filled in a sample portion of each chart, so you can really see the process in action. These charts are designed to be photocopied and used as hard copy. The back of each paper will be blank, providing a great place to write notes or if you recycle your paper like I do, the page can be reprinted with the next project in mind.

For those of you who are so computer savvy that you have all your files backed up to some external hard drive and to an Internet website and also use Excel to keep your stuff together, then this book is not for you. For the rest of us writers who are often so deep into the creative process that we sometimes forget to eat, this book should help you keep your feet on the ground while your mind is off having fun in the clouds.

Article Information Chart

When thinking of an article you want to write, it's helpful to know the target market.

With this chart, you can write down the publication you want to query, the tone and

style of the publication, the main points you want to use in your article and even

generate thoughts for that first, very important opening paragraph.

Article Information

Article Headline: _Five Easy Steps to Overcome Writer's Block_

For Publication: _Ditched the Niche Blog_

Publication Tone and Style: _Practical advice / Upbeat, spunky_

Estimated Word Count: _1200_

Main Points to Include

1. _Exercise_

2. _Read_

3. _Visit a bookstore_

4. _____

5. _____

Lede Paragraph

Article Information

Article Headline: _____

For Publication: _____

Publication Tone and Style: _____

Estimated Word Count: _____

Main Points to Include

1._____

2._____

3._____

4._____

5._____

Lede Paragraph

Research Notes

Article Submissions Chart

Once you've come up with an idea for an article, you'll need to keep track of where you've sent your queries. This chart will help you stay organized. And once your article idea has been accepted, you can write down all the final details so you'll know the date the piece is due, the amount you'll be paid, and other pertinent information.

Article Submissions

Title of Work: _Five Easy Exercises to Do at the Office_

Magazine Title	Women's Health Magazine
Contact Person	Jane Doe
Address	400 South 10th Street, Emmaus PA 18098
E-mail Address	womenshealth@rodale.com
Date Submitted	3-2-2013
Method of Submission	e-mail
Response: Y/N/Date	

Magazine Title	
Contact Person	
Address	
E-mail Address	
Date Submitted	

Article Submissions

Title of Work: _____

Magazine Title	
Contact Person	
Address	
E-mail Address	
Date Submitted	
Method of Submission	
Response: Y/N/Date	

Magazine Title	
Contact Person	
Address	
E-mail Address	
Date Submitted	
Method of Submission	
Response: Y/N/Date	

Magazine Title	
Contact Person	
Address	
E-mail Address	
Date Submitted	
Method of Submission	
Response: Y/N/Date	

Upon Acceptance

Contract and Payment Details: _____

Due Date for Finished Materials: _____

Date Sent Finished Piece: _____

Date of Payment: _____

Date of Publication: _____

Notes: _____

_____

_____

_____

Bibliography Chart

If you're writing any kind of nonfiction piece that uses references, you'll want to include a bibliography in the back of your book. This chart helps you keep track of the books you've referenced and is set up so that the proper format is used. Just remember to put the author's name with the last name first, then the first name.

Bibliography

Author Editor	Title	City	Publisher	Date
Sambuchino, Chuck	Create Your Writer Platform	Cincinnati	Writer's Digest Books	2012
Selgin, Peter	179 Ways to Save a Novel	Cincinnati	Writer's Digest Books	2010
McNally, John	Vivid and Continuous: Essays and Exercises for Writing Fiction	Iowa City	University of Iowa Press	2013

Bibliography

Author Editor	Title	City	Publisher	Date

Book Review Information Chart

When I receive a book to review, it is helpful to write down all the information on
the book in one location. I also include any possible quotes I may wish to use in the
review, so that I can write the review with ease.

Book Review Information

Book Title: _Bird Box_

Author: _Josh Malerman_

ISBN: _9780062259653_

Publisher: _Ecco_

Price: _$25.99_   **Format:** _Hardcover_

Publication Date: _May 13, 2014_

Page Number	Possible Quote to Use
1	"The Children sleep under chicken wire draped in black cloth down the hall"
2	"This was once a nice house in a nice suburb of Detroit… But this morning, the windows are covered with cardboard and wood."

Book Review Information

Book Title: _____

Author: _____

ISBN: _____

Publisher: _____

Price: _____ **Format:** _____

Publication Date: _____

Page Number	Possible Quote to Use

Book Reviews Chart

I write book reviews on a monthly basis, and this chart helps me keep track of what books I've received for review. I can also note the day the book arrived and when it is due (anywhere from two weeks to a month after arrival), and to whom I am sending the review. I also like to know how much I received in payment and the date the payment arrived, so if something gets lost in the mail, or an editor happens to forget to pay me, I can gently nudge them for payment.

Book Reviews

Book Title / Author	Arrival Date / Due Date	Submitted to:	Payment: Amount/Date
Wanted Women / Debrah Scroggins	Oct 17 2011 / Nov. 17, 2011	Christian Science Monitor	$150.00 / Feb. 2, 2012
La Tartine Gourmand / Beatrice Peltre	Nov. 1 2011 / Nov. 15, 2011	Foreword Reviews	$30.00 / Feb. 6, 2012
Grow Girl / Heather Donahue	Oct 1, 2012 / Oct 15, 2012	High Times	$50.00 / Jan 4, 2013

Book Reviews

Book Title Author	Arrival Date Due Date	Submitted to:	Payment: Amount/Date
-------------------	-------------------		-------------------
-------------------	-------------------		-------------------
-------------------	-------------------		-------------------
-------------------	-------------------		-------------------
------------------- -------------------	-------------------		-------------------
-------------------	-------------------		-------------------

Brainstorming Chart

Many times, I like to use this type of chart to generate new ideas. If I start with a general concept in the largest circle, then I can work outward toward all the other boxes. I may not use all the ideas this type of exercise generates, but it's good to have them down on paper in case I do decide to use them.

Brainstorming Chart

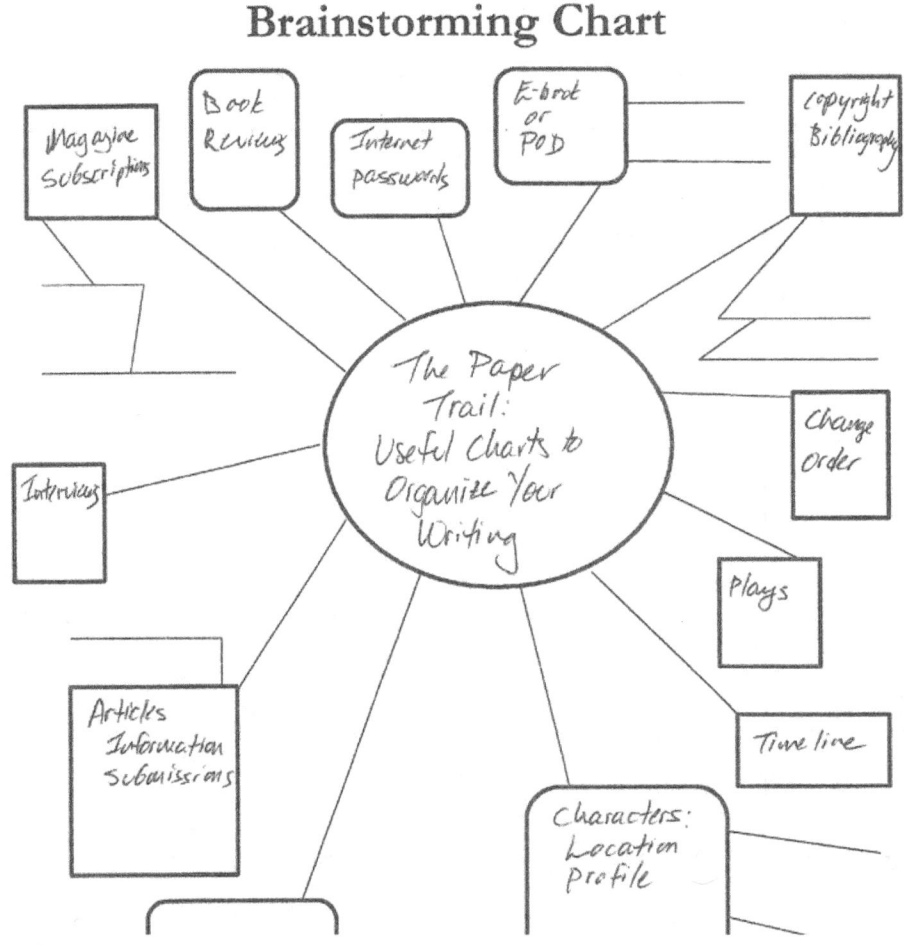

Brainstorming

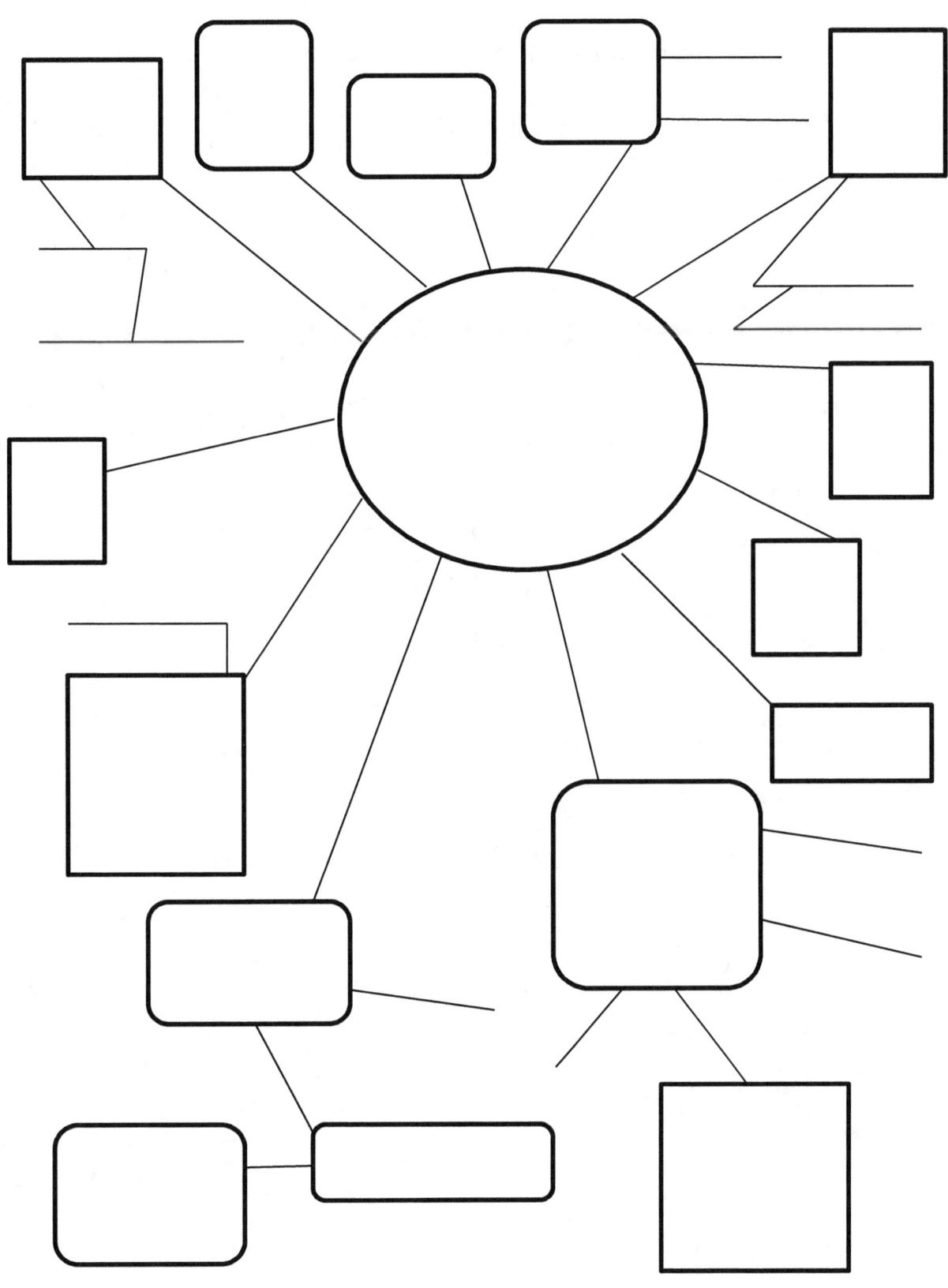

Business Deductions Chart

As a freelance writer, it's important to keep track of the many things you can deduct off your taxes. This chart should help you monitor your weekly and monthly expenses, so come tax time, the information is ready to be filed on the appropriate IRS form.

Business Deductions: Tax Year _2012_

Expense	Weekly	Monthly	Total
Advertising	$25.00		1300.00
Car/Truck			
Commissions and Fees			
Contract Labor			
Depletion			
Depreciation			
Insurance		$69.00	$828.00
Legal Services			
Magazine Subscriptions			
Memberships			
Mortgage Interest			
Office Supplies		$45.00	$540.00
Pension Plans			
Rent or Lease		$600.00	$7200.00
Repairs and Maintenance			
Supplies			
Taxes and Licenses			
Travel: Meals Entertainment			
Utilities		$125.00	$1500.00
Wages			

Business Deductions: Tax Year_____

Expense	Weekly	Monthly	Total
Advertising			
Car/Truck			
Commissions and Fees			
Contract Labor			
Depletion			
Depreciation			
Insurance			
Legal Services			
Magazine Subscriptions			
Memberships			
Mortgage Interest			
Office Supplies			
Pension Plans			
Rent or Lease			
Repairs and Maintenance			
Supplies			
Taxes and Licenses			
Travel: Meals Entertainment			
Utilities			
Wages			
Other Expenses			

Change Order Chart

Congratulations, you have a freelance client who wants you to write for them. You start preparing the work according to your signed contract. And then, all of a sudden, they ask for changes. Well, my friend, you want to make sure you have those changes written down on paper with a signature from the person who hired you, so if there's any question down the road as to why you wrote what you did, you can say, "Hey, let's look at the change order that I have right here."

Change Order

Client	J. Fowles
Contact Information	123 Main St. / jfowles@gmail.com
Project Title	The Pyramid Factor
Project Number	04072013
Date	May 9, 2013

Description of Change:
1. Change the footnotes to endnotes
2. add four more titles to the bibliography
3. indent quotes ten spaces and justify

Schedule for Change:
1. By May 22
2. By May 23
3. By May 31

Budget	additional $300.00
Approved: Y | N	Yes

Change Order

Client	
Contact Information	
Project Title	
Project Number	
Date	

Description of Change:

Schedule for Change:

Budget	
Approved: Y | N	
Client Signature	
Date Signed	
Notes	

Chapter Synopsis Chart

Whether you do it while you're writing your novel or after the novel is written, more than likely, you'll need to create a synopsis of your work. This chart will help you track your book chapter by chapter, so that when it comes time to write the actual synopsis, all the information is at hand. Most agents and publishers want to see a full, several-page synopsis, but this is also useful for a one-page, hit-the-main-highlights summary as well.

Chapter Synopsis: Title of Work: _Born in the Wayeb_

Chapter	Character(s)	Main Event	Notes
One	Satal Sachoj	Satal summons the gods of the Underworld to enter Mayapán.	First night of the Wayeb
Two	Yatal Ajkun Chiman	Yatal helps Ajkun birth his daughter and turns his back on her.	Last night of the Wayeb

Chapter Synopsis: Title of Work: _____

Chapter	Character(s)	Main Event	Notes

Character Location Chart

When you're writing a long novel and have many characters in the story like in

George R.R. Martin's popular series, *A Song of Fire and Ice*, it's helpful to have a chart

that keeps track of where each character is located. Or perhaps you're writing a

murder mystery and want to remember where each suspect is introduced since you

don't want to present information that relates to that character if he or she hasn't

appeared in the story line yet.

Character Location: Title of Work _Born in the Wayb_

Name of Character	Chapter	Chapter	Chapter	Chapter	Chapter	Chapter
Yakal	2	5	9			
Chiman	2	7	14			
Satal	1	3	8			
Ajkun	2	4	12			

Name of Character	Chapter	Chapter	Chapter	Chapter	Chapter	Chapter

Character Location: Title of Work_____

Name of Character	Chapter	Chapter	Chapter	Chapter	Chapter	Chapter

Name of Character	Chapter	Chapter	Chapter	Chapter	Chapter	Chapter

Name of Character	Chapter	Chapter	Chapter	Chapter	Chapter	Chapter

Character Profiles Chart

Once you have an idea in your head for a short story or novel, it's helpful to get to know your characters before you start writing. Who are the people you intend to introduce to your readers? What do they like to eat or drink? Do they have a favorite book or piece of music? Do they have any hobbies? You may not need to fill in all the blanks, or you may need to add more information depending on how well you want to know your characters before you start writing.

Character Profiles: Title of Work _Born in the Cayeb_

	Character One	Character Two	Character Three	Character Four
Name	Na'om	Satal		
Role in story	protagonist	antagonist		
Age	15	52		
Residence	Pa nima´	Mayapán		
Physical description	black hair brown eyes	gray hair wrinkles short - 4 ft.		
Occupation	trainee for herbal medicine	member of city council		
Education				
Favorite Food	tamales	boiled lizard		
Favorite				

Character Profiles: Title of Work_____

	Character One	Character Two	Character Three	Character Four
Name				
Role in story				
Age				
Residence				
Physical description				
Occupation				
Education				
Favorite Food				
Favorite Beverage				
Favorite Author				
Favorite Music				
Biggest Fear				
Personality Type				
Hobbies				
Notes				

Copyright Permissions Chart

When you've quoted someone else's work in your own work, unless the quotes are very short, you will need to request permission from the publisher to include these comments in your own manuscript. Unfortunately, most places won't give you permission until you have a publisher lined up for your manuscript. When you've reached that stage, you'll need to know the exact page number and words you're quoting as well as all the pertinent information about your soon-to-be-published masterpiece. This chart helps you keep track of all those nitpicky details.

Copyright Permissions

Information about Your Book:

Title of book: _Born in the Wayeb_

Publisher: _XYZ Publishing_

Format: Print: _X_ Electronic: _X_ Audio: _____ Internet: _____

Price: _16.95_ Publication Date: _11|08|2014_ Number of Pages: _334_

Information about Their Book:

Title of book: _A Guide to Mexican Witchcraft_

Author/Editor/Translator: _William and Claudia Madsen_

Publisher/Imprint: _Minutiae Mexicana_

ISBN: _114-210-007-6294_

Page Number	Specific Quoted Material
87	The healer: well versed in herbs, who knows through experience the roots, the trees, the stones.

Copyright Permissions

Information about Your Book:

Title of book:_____

Publisher:_____

Format: Print:_____ **Electronic:**_____ **Audio:**_____ **Internet:**_____

Price:_____ **Publication Date:**__|__|_____ **Number of Pages:**_____

Information about Their Book:

Title of book:_____

Author/Editor/Translator:_____

Publisher/Imprint:_____

ISBN:_____

Page Number	Specific Quoted Material

E-book or Print-on-Demand Layout Chart

You've written a book, and you've decided to sell it as an e-book and/or a print-on-demand book. But now comes the tricky part—what do you have to include to make this manuscript into a book? You can't just submit a bunch of chapters. You'll need to add the front matter, the back matter, and other necessary details. Note: If you're the author, you don't need to fill this section out, but if you do formatting for a client, you'll want to record this information.

E-book or Print on Demand Layout

Title: _The Paper Trail_			
Subtitle: _Useful Charts to Organize Your Writing_			
Author: _Lee E. Cart_			
Font: Style and Size	Title: _Garamond, Bold, 24 pt._ Subtitle: _Garamond, Bold 20 pt._ Chapter Headings:		
Margins: _1" all around + .13" for gutter_		Trim Size: _8.5 x 11_	
Pages to Include:			
Copyright	✓	Appendix	
Also By	✓	Chronology	
Dedication	✓	Abbreviations	
Epigraph		Notes	
Table of Contents		Glossary	
List of Illustrations		List of Contributors	
List of Tables		Illustration Credits	

E-book or Print-on-Demand Layout

Title:	
Subtitle:	
Author:	

Font: Style and Size	Title: Subtitle: Chapter Headings:

Margins:	Trim Size:

Pages to Include:

Copyright		Appendix	
Also By		Chronology	
Dedication		Abbreviations	
Epigraph		Notes	
Table of Contents		Glossary	
List of Illustrations		List of Contributors	
List of Tables		Illustration Credits	
Foreword		Index	
Preface		Notes:	
Acknowledgments			
Introduction			
Prologue			
About the Author			

Glossary of Terms Chart

If you've written a book that contains foreign terms or created a language for your

characters, it can be helpful to the reader to have a glossary to refer to when they've

forgotten the meaning of a phrase.

Glossary of Terms

Foreign Term	English Equivalent	Located on Page
ati't	An affectionate term for grandmother	7
balché	A fermented, honey-sweetened drink made from tree bark	27
copal	an aromatic tree resin burned as incense	12

Glossary of Terms

Foreign Term	English Equivalent	Located on Page

Income Chart

Once you've started to generate an income as a freelance writer, you'll want a way to keep track of your income, especially when it comes time to pay taxes on the amount you've earned. Hopefully, you'll have to use many of these charts for the year!

Income for Year: _2013_

Date Paid	Description of Work	Amount Paid	Notes
1/4/2013	Book review	$50.00	
1/18/2013	Book reviews	$200.00	
1/21/2013	editing work	$700.00	
1/31/2013	editing work	$435.00	

Income for Year: _____

Date Paid	Description of Work	Amount Paid	Notes

Internet Addresses and Password Chart

It's not wise to save all your Internet passwords on your computer. If you are hacked, your passwords are bound to be one of the first things a hacker scans your personal information for so they can gain access to all your online activities and accounts. I prefer to have a hard copy of my information that I keep readily available. When my computer crashed on me, I discovered I had lost all my bookmarked Internet sites, so this chart helps me keep track of those URLs, just in case I need to replace them in the future.

Internet Addresses and Passwords

Webpage Name	The Freelance Writer's Den
URL	freelancewritersden.com
Login	jsmith.com
Password/PIN	xxxxxxxx
Security Question/Answer	Favorite animal? Bear

Webpage Name	Firepole Marketing
URL	firepolemarketing.com
Login	jsmith.com
Password/PIN	xxxxxxxx
Security Question/Answer	Name of high school? Evergreen

Webpage Name	
URL	

Internet Addresses and Passwords

Webpage Name	
URL	
Login	
Password/PIN	
Security Question/Answer	

Webpage Name	
URL	
Login	
Password/PIN	
Security Question/Answer	

Webpage Name	
URL	
Login	
Password/PIN	
Security Question/Answer	

Webpage Name	
URL	
Login	
Password/PIN	
Security Question/Answer	

Webpage Name	
URL	
Login	
Password/PIN	
Security Question/Answer	

Notes

Invoice Chart

I use this chart for my own records, so I can keep track of the work I've done for a

client. When it comes time to create an invoice to send to that client, on my official

letterhead paper, I can refer to this chart for the information I need.

Invoice

Client Name:	Title of work:		Rate of Pay:	
Fowles, J.	Belief		$35.00/hr.	

Date	Description of Work	Hours	Total
1/8/14	editing and endnotes	4	$140.00
1/9/14	editing and endnotes	3.5	$122.50
1/16/14	import new illustrations + edits	2.5	$87.50
1/17/14	editing and endnotes	5	$175.00

Invoice

Client Name:	Title of work:		Rate of Pay:	
Date	Description of Work		Hours	Total

List of Ideas Chart

After I've used the Brainstorming Chart, I often use this chart to place my ideas into the various categories where I think they might fit. I can refer to this information when I am ready to start a new project and don't lose track of my ideas. They just percolate on the back burner until I can get to them. I've left room for you to add your own project categories.

List of Ideas

	Idea	Title
Essay	Birth of son	You Better Look Again
Short Story		
Poem	Mayan sacrifice	Maya Blue
Magazine Article		
Blog Post		
Play		
Newspaper article		
White paper		
Fiction book	Historical fantasy set in ancient Mayan times	Born in the Wayeb
Nonfiction book		
Graphic novel		

List of Ideas

	Idea	Title
Essay		
Short Story		
Poem		
Magazine Article		
Blog Post		
Play		
Newspaper article		
White paper		
Fiction book		
Nonfiction book		
Graphic novel		

Magazine Subscription Chart

Okay, I'll be the first to admit it, I'm addicted to magazines. I love the feel of the glossy paper, the bright and colorful photographs, and the information I acquire when I read the articles. Because I subscribe to so many magazines, it's hard to remember when that particular subscription is up for renewal, especially since the magazine companies like to send renewal notices up to six months before they are due! Now when I receive a renewal notice, I check my chart, and if I still have several months left on my order, I drop their request in the recycle bin.

Magazine Subscriptions

Name of Magazine	Date of Renewal	Number of Years	Amount	Notes
Outdoor Photographer	12-15-13	1 yr.	14.97	
Travel + Leisure	2-21-14	1 yr.	19.95	
MORE	4-4-14	1 yr.	15.00	gift subscription to Dawie

Magazine Subscriptions

Name of Magazine	Date of Renewal	Number of Years	Amount	Notes

Mileage Chart

If you do any driving connected with your freelance writing business, you need to

keep track of the miles you accrue, since mileage is considered a business expense.

Mileage

Date	From	To	One-way Mileage	Total Mileage	Tolls
1/16/14	house	J. Fowlis	40	80	0
2/26/14	house	B+N	65	130	$2.00
3/1/14	house	J. Fowlis	40	80	0
3/15/14	house	PO	7	14	0

Mileage

Date	From	To	One-way Mileage	Total Mileage	Tolls

Online Job Applications Chart

Nowadays, many freelancers find all their work online. This chart helps you track who you've contacted, when you contacted them, the rate of pay, the description of the job, the documents you sent, and other pertinent details. With all of this written down, you can make sure you follow up on your application in a timely manner.

Online Job Applications

Date Submitted Application	8/5/13
Contact Person	A. Rice
E-mail Address.	arice@gmail.com
Description of Job	memoir editor
Pay Rate	$30/hr
Subject Line Information	Memoir Editor
Documents Included	Résumé, clips
Response: Y/N/Date	Y/8/25/13
Notes	needs developmental advice

Date Submitted Application	
Contact Person	

Online Job Applications

Date Submitted Application	
Contact Person	
E-mail Address	
Description of Job	
Pay Rate	
Subject Line Information	
Documents Included	
Response: Y/N/Date	
Notes	

Date Submitted Application	
Contact Person	
E-mail Address	
Description of Job	
Pay Rate	
Subject Line Information	
Documents Included	
Response: Y/N/Date	
Notes	

Date Submitted Application	
Contact Person	
E-mail Address	
Description of Job	
Pay Rate	
Subject Line Information	
Documents Included	
Response: Y/N/Date	
Notes	

Play Details Chart

I know a few people who write plays and have them produced by local theater groups. Someday I want to write a play and when I do, I'll use this chart to help me organize my thoughts.

Play Details

Title of Play: _What's in a Name?_

Characters: _Mark – lead male_
April – lead female

Time: _2044_
Place: _NYC_
Setting: _Central Park, Met., apartment_

Act _One_		
Scene One	**Scene Two**	**Scene Three**
In the apartment _Mark + April –_		
Act_____		
Scene One	**Scene Two**	**Scene Three**

Play Details

Title of Play: _____

Characters: _____

_____

_____

_____

Time: _____

Place: _____

Setting: _____

_____

Act_____		
Scene One	**Scene Two**	**Scene Three**

Act_____		
Scene One	**Scene Two**	**Scene Three**

Poetry Contest Submissions Chart

If you're a poet and you're trying to get your work published in a variety of literary journals or magazines, it's helpful to keep track of what poems you sent where so you don't wind up sending out duplicates. Many journals will allow you to submit a group of poems, which is why I included spaces for up to five poems.

Poetry Contest Submissions

Contest Name	The 2014 Rattle Poetry Prize
Publication	Rattle
Address	
E-mail address	http://www.rattle.com/poetry
Deadline	July 14, 2014
Fee	$20.00
Prize or award	$5000 + publication
Date of submission	May 1, 2014
Title of poem	Maya Blue
Title of poem	Yaguar
Title of poem	Sister Act
Title of poem	
Title of poem	
Response: Y/N/Date	
Notes	

Contest Name	
Publication	

Poetry Contest Submissions

Contest Name	
Publication	
Address	
E-mail address	
Deadline	
Fee	
Prize or award	
Date of submission	
Title of poem	
Title of poem	
Title of poem	
Title of poem	
Title of poem	
Response: Y/N/Date	
Notes	

Contest Name	
Publication	
Address	
E-mail address	
Deadline	
Fee	
Prize or award	
Date of submission	
Title of poem	
Title of poem	
Title of poem	
Title of poem	
Title of poem	
Response: Y/N/Date	
Notes	

Publishers and Their Imprints Chart

When you use many quotations in a book, you'll need to request permission from the publishers to use those quotes. Many imprints are actually just smaller parts of a larger publishing house, which is who you'll need to contact for permission. This chart helps you organize your books by imprint so that you can request permission for all the quotes from that giant publishing house at once, regardless of the imprint under which the book may have been published.

Publishers and Their Imprints

Book Title	Author	Publishing House/Imprint
Seth Speaks	Jane Roberts	Random House/ Bantam
Boundaries of the Soul	June Singer	Random House/ Doubleday
Psyche + Symbol	C. G. Jung	Random House/ Doubleday/Anchor

Publishers and Their Imprints

Book Title	Author	Publishing House/Imprint

Social Media Schedule Chart

We all know how important it is to maintain a presence online via social media. It's important for readers to see your name on your blog posts, your Twitter feed, your Facebook page devoted to your writing, etc. But if you're like me, you're also extremely busy writing and doing a thousand other things, so you sometimes forget to post or Tweet or "like" something. This chart helps you stay on track by providing a place to check off each social media spot. You certainly don't have to use them all or use them every day, but with a little organization, you'll be able to plan which site you need to visit next. And yes, there are only twenty-eight days on this chart, so that you take a day or two off in any given month.

Social Media Schedule

Month: _May_

	Sun	Mon	Tues	Wed	Thurs	Fri	Sat
Blog	X			X			
Facebook	.	X			X		
Goodreads			X				
Google+							
LinkedIn		X		X		X	
Pinterest	X						X
Twitter	X	X	X	X	X	X	X
YouTube						X	

	Sun	Mon	Tues	Wed	Thurs	Fri	Sat
Blog							
Facebook							
Goodreads							
Google+							
LinkedIn							
Pinterest							

Social Media Schedule: Month: _____

	Sun	Mon	Tues	Wed	Thurs	Fri	Sat
Blog							
Facebook							
Goodreads							
Google+							
LinkedIn							
Pinterest							
Twitter							
YouTube							

	Sun	Mon	Tues	Wed	Thurs	Fri	Sat
Blog							
Facebook							
Goodreads							
Google+							
LinkedIn							
Pinterest							
Twitter							
YouTube							

	Sun	Mon	Tues	Wed	Thurs	Fri	Sat
Blog							
Facebook							
Goodreads							
Google+							
LinkedIn							
Pinterest							
Twitter							
YouTube							

	Sun	Mon	Tues	Wed	Thurs	Fri	Sat
Blog							
Facebook							
Goodreads							
Google+							
LinkedIn							
Pinterest							
Twitter							
YouTube							

Source Information Chart

You have a great idea for an article or long blog post, but your editor wants to make sure you interview an expert on the topic and include that information in your piece. This chart provides a space to write all the interviewee's contact information as well as the questions you might ask during the interview and the corresponding answers.

Source Information

Full Name	J. Thomas
Full Job Title	retired school teacher
Name of Business	N/A
Address	123 Main St. Portland ME
E-mail Address	jthomas123@gmail.com
Phone Numbers: Business | Cell	
Brief Bio and Description: retired school teacher, sixty-eight, 5'10", long hair went to UConn, lives off-the-grid	
Relevant Data: Age | Name of Kids	
Date of Contact	3/1/08
Contacted Via: Phone | E-mail | Other	e-mail / in person
Question: Why did you protest against the Vietnam War?	**Answer:** We shouldn't have been in Vietnam at that time.
Question:	**Answer:**

Source Information

Full Name	
Full Job Title	
Name of Business	
Address	
E-mail Address	
Phone Numbers: Business|Cell	
Brief Bio and Description:	
Relevant Data: Age| Name of Kids	
Date of Contact	
Contacted Via: Phone|E-mail|Other	
Question:	**Answer:**
Question:	**Answer:**
Question:	**Answer:**
Question:	**Answer:**
Question:	**Answer:**

Style Sheet Chart

If you do any kind of freelance editing, it's important to follow certain standards of formatting. These may be determined by the editing company you're working for or you may follow a style guidebook like *The Chicago Manual of Style*. This chart helps you remember the particular details for the individual manuscript you're working on. There's nothing worse than reading seventy-five pages of text and then wondering if the main character's name is spelled Halen or Haylen or if the author wanted a particular word capitalized throughout the text.

Style Sheet

Headings: Typeface and Size ___TNR 18 pt___
Body Text: Typeface and Size ___TNR 12 pt___
Layout of Sections: _____
Line Spacing: ___double___   Margin Width: ___1" all around___
Spacing between Headings: ___two___

Individual Words

Capitalized	Italicized	Hyphenated	Special Spelling
Source		mind-body	Haylen
River		mind-soul	Jack-e
The One			

Style Sheet

Headings: Typeface and Size _____

Body Text: Typeface and Size _____

Layout of Sections: _____

Line Spacing: _____   Margin Width: _____

Spacing between Headings: _____

Individual Words

Capitalized	Italicized	Hyphenated	Special Spelling

Submissions to Agents Chart

Once you've written a manuscript and revised it to perfection, it's time to send it out to agents. Since many agents take several weeks to respond, it's good to continue sending out those queries while you wait. This chart helps you remember all the pesky details for each submission.

Submissions to Agents

Title of work: _Born in the Wayeb_

Agent	Kristin Nelson
Agency	Nelson Literary Agency
Contact Address ·	—
E-mail Address	query@nelsonagency.com
Query | Synopsis | First____ Pages	Query only
Date Sent | Response:Y | N | Date	2/17/14 – 2/18/14 No
Notes	Form letter
Agent	Linda Epstein
Agency	Jennifer De Chiara Lit. Agency
Contact Address	—
E-mail Address	linda.p.epstein@gmail.com
Query | Synopsis | First____ Pages	Query, 1 Pt synopsis, bio, 20 pgs
Date Sent | Response:Y | N | Date	2/25/14 – 3/28/14 No
Notes	Form letter
Agent	
Agency	
Contact Address	
E-mail Address	

Submissions to Agents

Title of work:_____

Agent	
Agency	
Contact Address	
E-mail Address	
Query | Synopsis | First_____ Pages	
Date Sent | Response:Y | N | Date	
Notes	

Agent	
Agency	
Contact Address	
E-mail Address	
Query | Synopsis | First_____ Pages	
Date Sent | Response:Y | N | Date	
Notes	

Agent	
Agency	
Contact Address	
E-mail Address	
Query | Synopsis | First_____ Pages	
Date Sent | Response:Y | N | Date	
Notes	

Agent	
Agency	
Contact Address	
E-mail Address	
Query | Synopsis | First_____ Pages	
Date Sent | Response:Y | N | Date	
Notes	

Agent	
Agency	
Contact Address	
E-mail Address	
Query | Synopsis | First_____ Pages	
Date Sent | Response:Y | N | Date	
Notes	

Three-Act Plot Structure Chart

When writing a novel, it's helpful to plot out the basic structure of your story. This is usually done in three parts. Here's a very brief overview. The opening is where the main character is introduced and the problem is presented, the middle is where all kinds of conflict occur while the main character struggles to overcome his or her problem, and the third part is the resolution.

Three-Act Plot Structure

Title: Born in the Wayeb
One Sentence Summary (25 words or less): A young Mayan woman born with the ability to foresee the future must sacrifice herself to save her village.
Major Themes: abandonment, sacrifice, faith in the unknown
Symbols and Motifs: blood sacrifices, birth, death, images of Mayan gods
Act One: Na'om is born at the end of the Wayeb. Her encounter with a jaguar proves her ability to foresee the future.
Act Two:

Three-Act Plot Structure

Title:

One Sentence Summary (25 words or less):

Major Themes:

Symbols and Motifs:

Act One:

Act Two:

Act Three:

Timeline Chart

When you're writing a memoir or a novel, and want to tie your story into the bigger picture of what was or is happening in the world, it's helpful to have a timeline available that lists the personal event with the corresponding world event.

Timeline

Date	Story Event	World Event
1503	Leonardo paints the Mona Lisa	St. Peter's Church started in Rome
1509	Leonardo returns to Milan after father's death	Henry VIII ascends English throne
1519	Leonardo dies	Cortez lands in Mexico

Timeline

Date	Story Event	World Event

To Do Chart

Okay, this chart is pretty obvious, but if you're like me, it's helpful to make daily and weekly to-do lists so you can stay on top of your work flow. Plus, crossing an item off the list always gives me a sense of accomplishment, regardless of the task.

To Do

Monday
~~e-mail John~~
~~e-mail CreateSpace~~
~~write heading and lede~~
~~work on new book~~

Tuesday
~~write article body~~
~~review notes on webinar~~
~~e-mail new client~~

Wednesday

To Do

Monday

Tuesday

Wednesday

Thursday

Friday

What If This Happens Chart

Sometimes when I'm writing, I get stuck. So, when I'm not sure how to move the plot forward, I'll pull out this chart and play around with possible ideas. If this happens, then this, this, or this will follow. It allows me to see potential avenues to explore without a lot of writing. And when I come up with a scenario I like, then I go back to my manuscript and work the idea into the storyline.

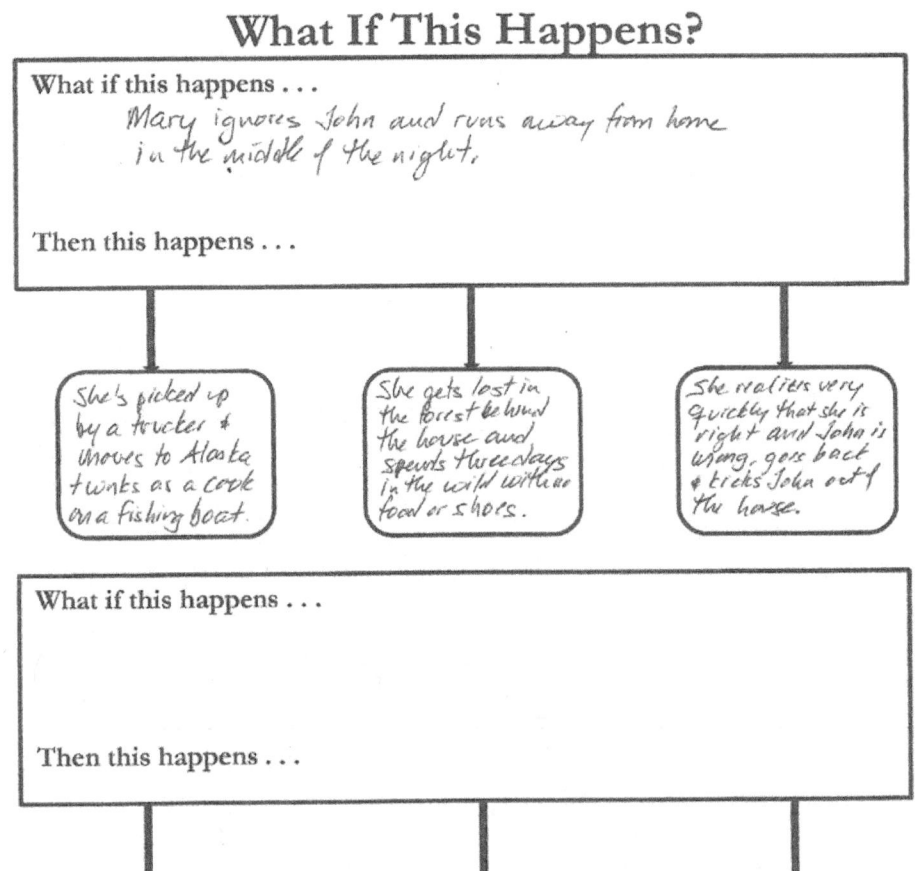

What If This Happens?

What if this happens . . .

Mary ignores John and runs away from home in the middle of the night.

Then this happens . . .

She's picked up by a trucker & moves to Alaska & works as a cook on a fishing boat.

She gets lost in the forest behind the house and spends three days in the wild without food or shoes.

She realizes very quickly that she is right and John is wrong, goes back & kicks John out of the house.

What if this happens . . .

Then this happens . . .

What If This Happens?

What if this happens . . .

Then this happens . . .

Notes

Workflow Chart

When I'm working on several projects at once, I find it's helpful to use this chart to monitor them. I can see at a glance which projects need my attention based on the due dates and can then transfer that information to my To-Do chart.

Workflow

Company Name ⇨	Shelf Awareness	Freelance A. Rice	Freelance J. Fowles		
Project and Due Date ⇩	Book Review Kinfolk Table 8/27/13	Chapter Eight 8/25/13	Chapter synopsis 8/23/13		
✍	Junkyard Planet Review 9/15/13	Chapter Nine 9/10/13	Bibliography 8/27/13		
✍	Our mathematical Universe Review 10/1/13	Chapter Ten 10/1/13	Endnotes 9/15/13		

Workflow

Company Name ⇨					
Project and Due Date ⇩					
✍					
✍					
✍					
✍					
✍					
✍					

Blank Charts

Now that you've had a chance to use the charts I created, you're bound to have

thought of some things you need to keep track of that are not included in this book.

So, I've provided you with two blank charts to use. Have fun!

Acknowledgments

This book would not have been possible without the constant support of my husband, Jeffrey Thomas, who always believes in me, loves me dearly, and thinks I'm beautiful, even on my worst days.

Thanks to my sister, Cher Michels, and her husband, Richard Procopio, for help in designing the book cover. And thanks to Angela DeRosa for her valuable feedback on the cover as it morphed through various permutations.

And thanks to all my writer friends and clients who have unknowingly contributed to this book. Because of my interactions with all of you, I had to learn how to stay organized as I moved from one project to another and thus, the idea of charts and a paper trail were born. Best of luck in your own writing.

About the Author

Lee E. Cart is a freelance writer, editor, and book reviewer. She is the author of *The Cracker Book: Artisanal Crackers for Every Occasion.* She lives off-the-grid in central Maine with her husband and two cats and can often be found in her organic garden when she's not busy working at her computer.